Original title:
Under the Hat's Shadow

Copyright © 2025 Creative Arts Management OÜ
All rights reserved.

Author: Adeline Fairfax
ISBN HARDBACK: 978-1-80586-050-1
ISBN PAPERBACK: 978-1-80586-522-3

Secrets of the Tipped Crown

Whispers float in the cool night air,
A wobbling crown with secrets to share.
Jesters giggle at the tales they spin,
Of some silly cat who chased after a fin.

Beneath a brim, a riddle lies,
Why does it tip when the chicken flies?
Crazy ducks in a feathered parade,
Setting the stage for a laugh that won't fade.

The Mystery Enshrined in Wool

A woolly tale tucked away with care,
A goat in slumber, dreaming of air.
Why does it snore with such strange delight?
Woolen whispers talk of a moonlit night.

Scarves that giggle when the cold winds blow,
A fluffy conspiracy no one should know.
With every stitch, a chuckle in line,
Knitting and laughing, oh how divine!

Fantasies Woven in Woolen Threads

Threads of laughter, woven so bright,
Knit together dreams that flicker with light.
A bunny hops with a mischievous grin,
While woolen fairies dance in a spin.

Patchwork stories that twirl and sway,
In the realm of the fuzzy, where pranks come to play.
Knots of joy tied with giggles and glee,
In every stitch, you'll find some spree.

The Curious Dance of Gentle Brim

A dance of hats with elegance rare,
Swirls and twirls in the summer air.
A slight little tip sends a giggle around,
As topsy-turvy hats take to the ground.

With every tip, the world comes alive,
In a joyful jig where hatters contrive.
Breezy capers, a funny parade,
All in good humor, no need to be weighed.

Whispers Beneath the Brim

A little birdie sang so sweet,
In a hat that's far from neat.
It chirps and tweets a funny tale,
Of socks misplaced and ships that sail.

Its brims hold secrets, what a sight,
Of missing snacks and cats in flight.
With every tip and every nod,
Laughter spills like a jolly pod.

Secrets of the Silken Crown

A crown of silk upon my head,
Where silly thoughts and dreams are fed.
It wiggles when the winds do blow,
And whispers of a dancing show.

In this regal fluff, I find delight,
It makes me twirl, it feels so right.
With every spin, the giggles grow,
As magic twirls in silly flow.

Beneath the Wide-Eyed Fabric

There's a fabric with a gaze so wide,
It winks at me, it won't abide.
It catches secrets, giggles galore,
As clowns and jesters dance on the floor.

Beneath this whimsy, laughter's found,
In mischief wrapped, a joy unbound.
Each fold's a tale so absurdly grand,
Of pratfalls and pies, oh so unplanned.

Enigma of the Dapper Veil

A dapper veil with charm and flair,
Hides a nosey gnome who lies in there.
He watches all with twinkling eyes,
As nutty pranks are on the rise.

With a tip and a twirl, he pulls a tease,
Tickling the toes, bringing us to our knees.
The fun unfolds like a playful riddle,
A laugh erupts, it can't be stifled.

Musings from a Cloaked Perspective

A cloaked figure shuffles near,
With secrets tucked, it's quite unclear.
Who's hiding there, in shadows cast?
A parade of oddities, unsurpassed.

Laughing hats with eyes like beads,
Rusty umbrellas sprout like weeds.
A curious dance of cloaks and ties,
Mystery blooms, as laughter flies.

Mysteries Entrapped in Woven Grace

A knitted riddle, full of twine,
Half-hidden jokes, all so divine.
With every stitch, a giggle brews,
In unraveling threads, there's much to muse.

Colors clasped, a vibrant show,
A spectacle that sways to and fro.
Who could predict the whimsy there,
In knitted knots, we dash and dare.

The Silent Persuasion of Fibrous Pride

A pompous thread with quite the flare,
Wags its tongue, if one should dare.
Each twisted fiber spins a jest,
Woven pride knows it's the best.

In cloth's embrace, the whispers dwell,
A tapestry of stories to tell.
Jovial fibers poke and pry,
In their embrace, we laugh and sigh.

Veils of Serenity and Mischief

A veil floats by, teasing the air,
With winks and nods, it has no care.
Whirlwinds dance with airy grace,
A jesting smile upon its face.

Between the folds, secrets ignite,
Witty puns take flight in the night.
A mischief maker, bright with glee,
In veiled delight, we're all set free.

Threads Woven Through Time

In a corner shop, quirky and bright,
A hat whispers tales, day and night.
Lost secrets of laughter, stitched with care,
Worn by the dreamers, floating through air.

Dapper gents tip their hats with flair,
While ladies giggle, tossing their hair.
Each fiber a story, each thread a rhyme,
We dance through the ages, spun out of time.

The Lure of the Brooding Brim

Oh, the brim that dips low, casting shadows so wide,
It draws in the curious, come look inside!
With a wink from the fabric, secrets arise,
A carnival of wonders, hidden from eyes.

Monocles and mustaches, they nod and they grin,
As the chatter grows louder, let the fun begin!
A riddle, a giggle, a pun here or there,
Across the brim's edge, laughter fills the air.

A Mosaic of Unspoken Whispers

Whispers cascade like soft summer rain,
Echoing softly, a sweet, silly strain.
Hats of all shapes, colors, and dreams,
Can launch a laugh riot, or so it seems.

The jester's cap teases, the bowler just grins,
While top hats spin tales of whimsical sins.
Underneath all the fabric, a free-for-all jest,
Where whimsy and giggles forever nest.

Hidden Laughter Beneath the Crown

Beneath a grand crown, the jests intertwine,
A throne of sweet chuckles, oh how they shine!
With each little toss, more laughter goes round,
In the kingdom of hats, joy's always found.

So come, gather 'round, heed the capricious call,
For under the coverings, there's fun for us all.
With each silly caper, each twist and each turn,
We'll dance through the shadows, where laughter must burn.

Reflections in a Stetson's Gaze

A Stetson's brim hides secrets true,
With silly thoughts that dance anew.
A rabbit peeks, then ducks from sight,
While giggles twirl in morning light.

A cowboy's wink, a playful tease,
He steals my sandwich, oh such a breeze!
The laughter echoes, a jolly jest,
In every fold, a wild quest.

Beneath that crown of rugged style,
Cheeky dreams emerge, stay awhile.
A lasso toss, a silly show,
As whimsy flows, we're free to glow.

With shadows stretching, jokes unite,
Beneath the gear, it's pure delight!
A tip, a touch, a light embrace,
In winks and grins, we find our place.

Veiled Thoughts of the Curious Mind

Beneath a cap, ideas play,
Like squirrels in a funny fray.
A twist of fate, a hat so wide,
It hides the dreams we try to ride.

A smirk appears, a twinkling eye,
With whispers shared, oh me, oh my!
The world's a stage, a joke or two,
A dance, a prance, we're all in view.

Peeking forth from fuzzy lines,
In hats, we find our silly signs.
Mirth runs wild, like banners high,
In droll reflections, we can fly.

From veils of thought, confusion reigns,
With chuckles echoing through the plains.
A laugh, a sight, a wink, a cheer,
In every shade, the joy is clear.

The Canvas of Hidden Dreams

A hat is more than fabric worn,
It's painted dreams, both bright and worn.
With colors splashed, a lively show,
It holds alive the joy we sow.

Sprinkled laughter, a canvas bright,
Each stroke a giggle, joy in flight.
With brushes made of wriggly thoughts,
In silly schemes, we find the spots.

From silly faces to wild hues,
The canvas whispers, a playful muse.
Underneath, where secrets romp,
The dreams emerge, all ready to stomp.

With every twist and turn so grand,
We paint with giggles, hand in hand.
A joyous heart, in dreams we play,
Our canvas glows, come what may!

Shadows Cast by a Feathered Crest

A feathered hat perched high and proud,
Hints of humor lost in the crowd.
A swish, a sway, it beckons me,
To dance with shadows, wild and free.

Jokes slip out and tumble near,
As laughter rings, oh sweet sincere!
In shadow play, the antics grow,
With every giggle, we steal the show.

A peek from under, a cheeky grin,
With fur-lined dreams that pull us in.
A feather's touch, a tickling breeze,
In silly games, we find our ease.

Cast in shapes that shimmer bright,
We stride and prance, oh what a sight!
Under the plume's embrace we find,
The joy of shadows, sweetly entwined.

Melodies in the Hidden Fold

A singer hides beneath a brim,
With a glance, the world is dim.
Each note that travels, leaps and bounds,
Making giggles from all around.

The pigeons dance, a feathery cue,
As if they know the tune is true.
Lopsided jokes weave through the air,
As laughter blooms without a care.

A top hat's tale of a bear so bright,
Sells ice cream cones that float in flight.
Juggling pineapples on a whim,
In a world where nothing is grim.

So take a step, don't be shy,
Join the fun as the moments fly.
In this strange place of silly sights,
Every shadow spins delightful nights.

In Search of Forgotten Echoes

Whispers linger in the breeze,
Tickling whispers that tease with ease.
An echo pops out, dressed in stripes,
Trading tall tales with laughing gripes.

Beneath the clamor of friendly cheer,
A squirrel debates if hats are queer.
With each decision, new sounds will bloom,
Filling the air like a sweet perfume.

Hats tell secrets of days gone by,
Of antics that made the old folks cry.
Frogs in bowties sing with delight,
As the moon giggles, glowing bright.

So flip your lid and spin around,
In silly phases of laughter found.
Each echo turns, still it remains,
Ticklish magic drives out the pains.

From the Depths of the Rims

Beneath the rims, a party brews,
With dancing shoes and a million views.
A snappy hat is where it's at,
As turtles twirl and don a spat.

Lollipops wear jester crowns,
As tickled socks dance through the towns.
Chickens cluck in a comical show,
Each feathered friend puts on a glow.

Juggling pies and dripping tea,
What a quirky sight to see!
Gags unfold like magic tricks,
As laughter rolls in cheerful flicks.

So marvel at the outlandish fun,
As shenanigans become the run.
Each rim reveals a cheeky glance,
Inviting you to join the dance.

In the Grasp of Twilight Textiles

Twilight whispers through the threads,
While pillow fights sprawled on beds.
With brightly stitched, peculiar dreams,
And giggles that burst at the seams.

Crazy fabrics twirl and spin,
Creating fashion where jokes begin.
A cat in a coat bows to the crowd,
Leaving all the passers-by wowed.

Tangled yarns weave tales untold,
Of socks that wear the brave and bold.
In every fold, a ticklish fear,
As whimsical mishaps draw near.

So shake a leg and tie a knot,
In this fabric world, give it a shot.
Where evenings burst with playful glee,
And make-believe runs endlessly.

Radiance from the Edge of Mystery

A curious hat perched high,
With secrets tucked inside.
It wobbles with the slightest breeze,
And makes the passerby slide.

A rabbit pops out on a whim,
With a wink and a cheeky grin.
He hands a carrot to a cat,
Who insists it's merely gin!

The brim's a portal, oh so grand,
To lands of fizzy drink and sand.
A twirl, a swirl, a sudden cheer,
As giggles spread across the land.

So tip your hat and take a chance,
For laughter leads the wiggly dance.
With mystery riding in the air,
Find joy in every silly prance.

Shades of Reveries Encapsulated

A hat that changes with the light,
Wears polka dots and stripes so bright.
Its feathers dance on breezy tales,
While socks debate on tiny scales.

Beneath it sleeps a sleepy snail,
Who dreams of cheese and earring mail.
A juggler jests with spoons of jam,
Says laughing's part of every plan!

With every tilt, a giggle flows,
As towel dolphins do their toes.
A twist, a turn, a twist again,
The hat's the best of all pretend!

Collect the shades of joyous glee,
Beneath the brim, let worries flee.
With whispers tickling ears so near,
A world of whimsy blooms right here.

A Knitted Tale of the Unseen

A knitted cap with tales untold,
Of purls and laughs, and yarn so bold.
It sprouted legs and danced for fun,
And chased a mouse who'd found the sun.

From stitches came a chorus bright,
Of playful puns in the soft twilight.
The needles tap a merry beat,
As silly socks all rise to greet.

The snickers spill from every seam,
As adventures weave a fuzzy dream.
With every loop, the humor grows,
While clowns wear hats of rainbow bows.

So grab your needles, spin a thread,
With joy unwrapped and laughter spread.
For every twist, a smile galore,
A tale of whimsy to explore.

The Benevolence of Threads Entwined

Threads of folly, colors bright,
In a hat that's quite a sight.
With buttons winking, eyes that twirl,
An invitation to a whirl.

A squirrel in shades of radiant hue,
Decides to join this crazy crew.
With every stitch, another cheer,
As yarn balls bounce without a fear.

The pattern twists with each new friend,
A tapestry that will not end.
With laughter echoed through the loom,
Creating joy that fills the room.

So wrap your heart in colors gay,
And let the threads then lead the way.
For every twist brings fun divine,
In this world of whims entwined.

The Quiet Realm of Fabric

In a realm where stitches play,
Lurking threads twirl and sway.
Buttons laugh in their own way,
As zippers giggle night and day.

A collar mutters, quite absurd,
While seams hold secrets, soft and blurred.
The cotton whispers all unheard,
In a space where voices go undeterred.

Tails of fabric weave a jest,
As patterns dance, they're quite the best.
With every fold, they're dressed to impress,
Each creased punchline brings a hearty fest.

So tip your hat to threads so bright,
For in their world, it's pure delight.
With laughter woven, pure and light,
Fabric frolics into the night.

Midnight Musings from Above

At midnight hour, hats take flight,
Whispering dreams in silver light.
Brimmed companions join the night,
In playful banter, quite a sight.

The fedoras tell a tale or two,
While beanies chuckle, feeling blue.
Each stitch a giggle, oh so true,
As midnight musings they pursue.

A top hat spins in a waltz so grand,
While sun hats stretch across the sand.
Each shadow molds a comical band,
Sharing laughs that never planned.

Through laughter's loom, the hours blend,
As hats unite, they won't pretend.
In the sky's embrace, no need to mend,
A night of chuckles, without end.

Beneath the Felted Veil

Beneath the veil of fabrics soft,
A world of whimsy, quite aloft.
Where woolly thoughts take flight and scoff,
And silly ideas spark and doff.

The felted friends join in a cheer,
With floppy ears, they lend an ear.
Tickling fancies, oh so near,
In this cozy realm, nothing's sheer.

Patchwork jests that softly chime,
Unraveling laughter, oh sublime.
In crazy quilt designs they climb,
Till giggles dance in perfect rhyme.

So don your felt with zest and glee,
In their warm company, you'll agree.
A tapestry of fun, wild and free,
Underneath, they hold the key.

The Hidden Stories of Twill

In the woven lanes where twill does slink,
Fabric whispers without a blink.
Each thread a tale, one neatly linked,
In patterns spun from playful ink.

Hounds tooth chuckles, plaid conspiracies,
Rustling whispers, woven mysteries.
With every fold, a jest that frees,
A secret dance that none can seize.

The denim skits in playful slides,
As twill giggles, where fun abides.
In every crease, a joy that hides,
Beneath each stitch, merriment glides.

So tread with joy on twill's fine ground,
Where laughter lives and joy abounds.
In fabric's tales, much can be found,
A patchwork life, laughter unbound.

Veils of Stardust and Dream

In a corner of the night,
A top hat danced with delight.
A rabbit peeked, oh so sly,
With winks and giggles passing by.

Feathers fluttered, a curious sight,
As dreams unfolded, taking flight.
A jester's grin, bright and wide,
In the stardust, secrets hide.

The moon chuckled, lifting high,
While shadows played, they'd never die.
Each twirl fetched a joyful cheer,
The world felt light, nothing to fear.

Laughter bounced off rooftops old,
In this realm where tales are told.
With hats so tall, they'd do a flip,
In the dreamscape, we took a trip.

The Curved Lid of Solitude

Beneath a lid of gleaming grace,
A wanderer found his jolly place.
With quirks and antics, he'd parade,
In solitude, his spirit played.

Twisting twirls, he made a mark,
His sneezes sounded like a lark.
In solitude's embrace, so grand,
He laughed at life, his playful stand.

The moon peeped in with a grin,
While shadows danced, suggesting sin.
Yet he embraced his quirky fate,
In solitude, he could create.

With every hat that bounced and swayed,
The universe applauded, unafraid.
In laughter's echo, he found delight,
A joyful heart within the night.

Echoes in the Cap's Embrace

Beneath the cap, a secret shared,
Whispers of humor, lightly bared.
Funny faces made by friends,
In a world where laughter never ends.

The echoes giggle, bounce and fly,
As antics mingle, oh my, oh my!
With every grin and charming jest,
The cap held wonders, never rest.

Juggling dreams and sprightly flair,
They wore their quirks without a care.
In every stitch, a memory spun,
The cap embraced, the laughter won.

Under twinkling stars they sang,
While silly songs made the night clang.
A tapestry of joy unfurled,
In the cap's embrace, they changed the world.

Shadows Among the Stitches

In the fabric where shadows dwell,
The stitches whispered, tales to tell.
With playful hearts and gleaming eyes,
They spun a yarn, oh what a surprise!

Each thread a spark of wild delight,
Where shadows dashed in playful flight.
They rolled and tumbled, what a scene,
In a cloak of laughter, bright and green.

The stitches danced, a lively crew,
While moments spun like morning dew.
Beneath, a world of dreams there swirled,
In the laughter's arms, they twirled.

With every knot and playful tease,
The fabric groaned and bent with ease.
In shadows bright, they flourished free,
A symphony of joy, pure glee.

Silhouettes of Memory Caught

In the corner lurks a fellow,
A whiskered cat in a bright yellow.
He chases dreams of fish and cream,
While we giggle, lost in a daydream.

A hat floats by, a ghostly wraith,
It tickles noses; it steals their breath.
With a flick and a flop, it's in the air,
What was that? A dance, oh what a flair!

Silly hats of every kind,
With quirks and jiggles, twists unwind.
They whisper tales of jesters past,
As they twirl around, we're all amassed.

So join the parade, let laughter unfold,
With hats and dreams, let's be bold.
In this realm where shadows play,
We twirl and spin, hip-hip-hooray!

A Dance of Thread and Thought

A seamstress sings with needle flying,
Stitch by stitch, she keeps on trying.
With colors bright and threads galore,
She weaves a tale we all adore.

Buttons bounce and zippers grin,
As the fabric dances, and we all spin.
It twirls in laughter, it leaps in cheer,
In this world, we lose all fear.

Patterns twist like jokes unspun,
Each layer hides a quirky pun.
Watch out! A patch might just take flight,
In this swirl of fabric delight.

So gather round, let's share this spree,
Of threads entwined in jubilee.
We'll stitch our stories, every seam,
In a patchwork joy, we'll live the dream.

The Mystery Beneath the Edge

There's a lid that wobbles on the ground,
What treasures lie beneath, we've found?
With a flourish and flip, let's take a peek,
    A parade of toys begins to speak!

A rubber chicken and a squeaky shoe,
They tango together while the crowd skews.
    Giggles arise as the curtain falls,
What mischief lies in those shadowed halls?

The edge of laughter teeters near,
With a playful whisper, it draws us here.
Shadows perform, their roles enacted,
In antics and winks, laughter is compacted.

So here we stand, on the brink of fun,
Where mystery and humor are never done.
With a nudge and a natter, let's set the stage,
    In the dance of shadows, we engage.

Hushed Entreaties of the Fabric

In the hush of the night, whispers weave,
Threads of laughter, they never leave.
Each fabric whisper, gentle, light,
Tickles the ears with tales of delight.

A patchwork quilt, a jester's hat,
Dancing in silence, imagine that!
With every fold, a joke is spun,
In this tapestry, we find our fun.

Colors clash and serendipity reigns,
While hooks and loops draw funny chains.
Behind the seams, secrets hide,
In the quiet, jovial hearts abide.

So stitch along, listen and churn,
With every giggle, let's brightly burn.
In the fabric of laughter, we entwine,
Creating a joy that's truly divine.

The Circular Reverie of Silhouette

A wide-brimmed wonder, oh what a sight,
A headpiece that dances in the moonlight.
With twirls and spins, it juggles the day,
    Creating good laughs in a silly way.

Peak-a-boo moments, where secrets are kept,
With shapes all around, the mind's keenly prepped.
A flick of the stitching, a dash of the seam,
    Leads to a laughter that mimics a dream.

The colors can chatter, they giggle and glow,
    Casting odd shadows, delightfully slow.
What tales do they whisper, oh what do they share?
As the brims keep on swaying, with whimsical flair.

So join in the fun, wear a hat of your own,
Join in the laughter, let silliness be shown.
The circular dance, oh please take a chance,
For life in this moment is all about prance.

Beneath the Ashen Shade

A cap with a story, so cozy and wide,
It blocks out the sunlight, like a magical ride.
Invisible gnomes with mischief in hand,
Whispering secrets only they understand.

The crows gather round, wearing tiny hats,
They plot little journeys with whimsical chats.
Figments appearing from the shadows so grand,
As they laugh at our fumblings, oh how they planned!

Silly encounters with dust bunnies roam,
In the quirkiest corners, they make themselves home.
The brim waves at passers, a nod to the fool,
For those in the know, find joy in the rule.

So sit for a while in this marvelous field,
With joy all around that's ready to yield.
The ashen glow brightens paths of delight,
Where laughter's the language from morning to night.

Stories Cradled in the Brim

A wobbly tale that's snug in its fold,
Where mischief is brewed and traditions retold.
Each layer a chapter, each corner a plot,
In an oversized cap, funny things are caught.

Underneath whispers of old, jovial lore,
Like kittens in hats who are eager for more.
A dance of the feathers, a spin of the thread,
Giving life to the stories that linger in dread.

Cradled in fabric, the giggles abound,
With stories so silly that whirl all around.
The brim holds the riddle, the secrets of cheer,
As everyone laughs and the fun draws near.

So let's write a tale with a marvelous twist,
In hats of adventure, let's make sure we persist.
For tales sung in laughter bring smiles to the brim,
And life is more vibrant when shared with a whim.

The Views from the Velvet Cap

A plush little piece that sits on the head,
With visions of mischief and fun oft misread.
A place for the giggles and chatter to play,
Where jokes may grow wings and flutter away.

The velvet surrounds, all warm and delight,
Capturing nonsense and sparking the night.
As whimsical thoughts leap like rabbits in spring,
While wearing this cap, one can feel like a king.

A peek through the rim sees the world upside down,
In laughter's embrace, we will never frown.
The cap grins in glee, as it sways to the beat,
Where the dance of the absurd makes life feel complete.

So grab on your velvet, in style, take a stand,
For views from this cap can be nothing but grand.
With laughter and stories, the nonsense runs free,
In this quirky adventure, just let yourself be.

Soliloquies of the Crescent Shade

A sneaky mouse danced with flair,
In a moonlit spot, without a care.
He spun in circles, oh what a sight,
While shadows grinned in the pale twilight.

A lonely hat hung upon a hook,
Whispering tales, oh come take a look.
Beneath the brim, secrets did flow,
Of giggling gnomes and a silly crow.

With a tilt and a twirl, the hat took flight,
Chased by a dog, oh what a delight!
They tumbled and rolled, both caught in glee,
In the shadows, laughing, just you wait and see.

So listen closely when night falls near,
To the hat's old stories, lend an ear.
For in its shade, laughter will bloom,
As fanciful antics dance in the gloom.

Light and Dark Beneath a Fabric Dome

In the corner, a sneaky cat lay,
With dreams of mischief in the light of day.
A fold of fabric, oh what a tease,
It whispered secrets with the gentlest breeze.

A sunbeam danced, sparkled in glee,
As the hat juggled shadows, oh, carefree!
Socks worn by clowns peeked out in fright,
Rustling with laughter and pure delight.

Underneath the brim, a party took place,
With a mouse, a frog, and a lopsided face.
They played hide and seek, quick as a dart,
With the hat as their stage, a true work of art.

At dusk, friends gathered to share their dreams,
Beneath laughs and giggles, and bright moonbeams.
For light and dark in a fabric dome,
Turned silly moments into a home.

Enigmatic Revelations from Stitched Silhouettes

A top hat sat, quite proud and tall,
With stitches that whispered a riddle to all.
Its shadow stretched, a mischievous grin,
As it plotted adventures that soon would begin.

With a wink and a nod, its secrets unfurled,
Of dancing squirrels and a cake that twirled.
Beneath those stitches, stories unwound,
Of a jester's pranks that joyously drowned.

A slapstick routine, all wrapped in thread,
As giggles erupted from dreams in their bed.
For every silhouette scripted anew,
A puzzle of laughter brought forth from the blue.

And as the night deepened, a chortle arose,
From the hat's shadow, where silliness flowed.
Enigmas tackled with a chuckle and shout,
In the land of stitched tales, come join in and spout!

Tapestry of Hushed Adventures

A silken thread weaves tales in the dark,
Of shoes that dance and dogs that bark.
With every fold, a giggle is spun,
A tapestry woven, where mischief is fun.

In corners hidden, secrets find light,
With whispers of jesters ready to bite.
A playful breeze tickles our toes,
As lighthearted mischief dances and grows.

Underneath the seams, a frog wears a crown,
While clowns juggle dreams in a whimsical town.
Their laughter twirls in the silence so sweet,
Creating a symphony of comical feet.

So gather 'round, let the stories unfold,
Of hush-hush adventures, both silly and bold.
For beneath each stitch lies a playful surprise,
In this tapestry bright, joy sparkles and flies!

Deliberations in a Shaded Retreat

Chin in hand, I sit and muse,
On sandwiches and secret clues.
The squirrels plot their little heist,
Their daring dreams served with iced rice.

My neighbor's hat is quite the sight,
Is it a cap or a fuzzy fright?
It twirls like a dancer in the breeze,
A marvel that makes the moment tease.

The gossip flies with laughter's gleam,
As we sip lemonade and scheme.
What flavors of whimsy shall we concoct?
I choose fancies, while others mock.

A rendezvous where whims collide,
With giggles shared and smiles wide.
In this nook, where nonsense lives,
The joy of friendship freely gives.

Echoes of the Pristine Arc

In the park where laughter swells,
A jester juggles unseen spells.
His hat is bright, his shoes a tease,
He's twirling tricks with such great ease.

Picnics sprout with vibrant glee,
As ants march forth with certainty.
They march in line, oh what a show,
To steal a crumb, they steal the glow.

The sun winks down on hats a-flying,
In this space, no one's sighing.
Chasing dreams of fancier snacks,
While pigeons plot their feathery attacks.

Here joy is light as summer's air,
With hat-toppers dancing without a care.
A swirl of fun, a shady mark,
Where every chuckle ignites a spark.

Veils of Gentility

Gentle laughs weave through the breeze,
As I sip tea with fragrant tease.
A dapper hat spins tales of woe,
Yet the laughter's pulse begins to grow.

The crumpets chat with their sweet delight,
As gossip slips into soft twilight.
With every nibble, a secret shared,
A dance of whim, perfectly paired.

In this realm of posh attire,
Where even the butterflies conspire.
The humor blooms, a rose in jest,
In hats where charm and laughter rest.

So let's toast to those in fancy threads,
Who tiptoe 'round and dance on heads.
For every giggle masks a quirk,
In this fine play where joy can lurk.

The Hushed Narratives of Elegance

Quiet whispers float through the air,
As hats adorn those unaware.
With every nod, a tale unfolds,
Of fanciful journeys and secrets bold.

A chap with a flair for the absurd,
Claims he found a talking bird.
But with each quip, the truth decays,
And laughter reigns in quirky ways.

Beneath these brims of tailored grace,
Life's comedy finds its friendly place.
We wink at the odd and cheer the bold,
In stories spun that never grow old.

So gather 'round this swanky scene,
With tales of whimsy that gleam and preen.
For in laughter's realm, we elevate,
Chasing joy, never hesitate.

Glimmers in the Dark Crown

A flicker of light, what could it be?
A squirrel in a bow tie, dancing with glee.
The moon's in a tux, shining so bright,
As shadows do prance, igniting the night.

With a grin, the owl hoots a loud joke,
While a cat wearing shoes sips on some smoke.
Beneath leafy whispers, the laughter ignites,
As friendships bloom softly in whimsical nights.

A Tapestry of Tales Unfolding

A pirate, a sage, a dragon in flight,
Gather 'round folks, it's storytime tonight!
With giggles and snorts, our voices do swell,
Each tale a grand journey, do come, find your spell!

There's a frog in a cloak, who dances with flair,
Holding court on a lily, without any care.
A princess in stripes, so bold and so bright,
Tricksters unite, in the warmth of moonlight.

The Unseen Weight of Wool

A sheep in a sweater, feeling quite grand,
Says, "Fashion is fun, oh isn't it bland?"
With a wink of an eye and a jump to the beat,
It twirls in a circle, so light on its feet.

But wait for a moment, the yarn's in a snare,
As a goat steals a stitch with an impish glare.
A tangled affair of laughter unbound,
In this cozy chaos, a new joy is found.

Reflections in the Broad Brim

Beneath a wide brim, a world does reside,
A jester with shoes that are floppy and wide.
With a flip and a flop, it dances away,
While shadows conspire to join in the play.

A fish in a fedora, now that's quite the sight,
Telling fish tales and adding delight.
With laughter, they whirl as the breeze takes its turn,
In the cozy embrace where the silliness churns.

A Duster's Secret Life

In a closet, tucked away,
A duster dreams of play.
It spins and twirls in glee,
Dancing with dust, carefree.

When the humans are not near,
It throws a grand frontier.
With feather friends, it prances,
Taking part in wild romances.

Around the chair, it twirls and slides,
Hiding secret dustball rides.
With every swish, it shouts out loud,
"I'm the softest of the crowd!"

But when the owner comes around,
Back to duty, it's tightly bound.
Yet at night, the story replays,
In duster dreams, it laughs and sways.

Dialogues from the Hushed Canopy

Underneath the leafy green,
A squirrel plots with a raccoon, keen.
"Let's find the biggest nut, my friend!"
"Yes, but we must not offend!"

From the branch, they schemed and planned,
While below, a dog didn't understand.
"You're chatting nuts? That's quite absurd!"
"But you, my friend, are just a bird!"

A wise owl swooped in with flair,
"Do you two need some fresh air?"
They laughed and whispered, oh so low,
"Just sharing secrets, don't you know?"

And thus, this canopy so grand,
Holds the quirkiest of a woodland band.
From giggles to chatter, all is merry,
Life in the trees is quite the cherry!

Whispers Beneath the Brim

A hat sits proud, atop a shelf,
With secrets held, it toys itself.
"What adventures have I seen?"
"Oh, more than you could ever glean!"

Beneath the brim, a mouse resides,
Countless tales of mischief, he confides.
"I've seen a cat dance on the floor!"
"With two left feet? I wish I saw more!"

The brim itself rolls back in laughter,
It's been a stage for many a dancer.
"Did you see the teapot spin?"
"Best show ever, let's do it again!"

Clatter and jingles, a party's begun,
As shadows play, and time's overrun.
On this shelf, the fun won't cease,
For every night brings sweet release.

Secrets of the Silk Band

A silk band rests on a vintage dress,
Whispers of parties, oh what finesse!
"I've been twirled at midnight balls,"
"And feasted where the chandelier falls!"

Each stitch a laugh, each thread a wink,
With sparkly tales that make you think.
"Do you recall the clumsy prince?"
"Who stumbled over his shoe, it makes no sense!"

They giggle softly, secrets to share,
As buttons listen with thoughtful care.
"One more dance before the night fades,"
"With jubilant spins in cloth cascades!"

As dawn approaches, tales will retract,
But the memories stay, a joyful pact.
For every garment needs its charm,
And the silk band spreads unrivaled warm.

Whirlwinds of Fabricated Thoughts

In a realm where fancies sprout,
Laughter dances all about.
A twirl of whimsy, a spin of dreams,
Ideas tumble, burst at the seams.

Jesters gather, hats tipped in jest,
While giggles illuminate the quest.
A thought so bright, it slips and glides,
Chasing shadows, where mirth abides.

With every twirl, the fabric frays,
We weave our tales in curious ways.
The absurdity, a joyful flight,
In a carnival of pure delight.

Secrets in the Band of Silence

Quiet whispers sneak around,
In the hush, the giggles abound.
A secret shared beneath the rim,
Tickles the toes, makes the head swim.

Muffled snickers in every nook,
A chuckle waits, just like a hook.
In silence, tales take on a shape,
Where silliness wears a fun-filled cape.

The stillness hides a playful grin,
As laughter brews from deep within.
In the lull, a joke makes its way,
Beneath the quiet, hilarity plays.

The Stolen Light Beneath the Fold

A soft glow glimpsed in a secret fold,
Where stories live, and giggles unfold.
Shadows beckon with a cheeky tune,
As sunlight pirouettes, and charms the moon.

Beneath the crease, a sparkle hides,
In every corner, laughter abides.
A heist of humor, oh what a plight,
Stealing brightness to banish the night.

The light tumbles, slips through the seams,
Creating chaos in our wild dreams.
With each chuckle, the world feels bright,
As stolen beams ignite the night.

Memories Stored in Stitched Shadows

In stitches, tales are sewn with glee,
Faded threads hold history.
With every knot, a giggle's sealed,
In shadows cast, the truth revealed.

Old hats whisper of past delights,
Of cheeky jests and merry sights.
Through seams of laughter, we find our way,
As the echoes of joy linger and sway.

Underneath the fabric's weave,
Silly moments we'll never leave.
With threads of humor, we stitch and bind,
Memories wrapped in laughter entwined.

The Archive of Fleeting Moments

In the attic of dreams, dust bunnies play,
A cat in a top hat sips tea all day.
Tickles and giggles in a box filled with care,
A note from the past whispers secrets so rare.

A mischievous sock makes a break for the door,
While rubber ducks waddle on the wooden floor.
Time ticks on softly, but laughter stays bold,
As a puppet parade tells tales long untold.

The Palette of Stowed Secrets

Colors collide in a jar of old paint,
A waltzing banana shimmies—oh, how quaint!
Brush strokes of laughter against walls that are bare,
Imagination runs wild, without a care.

Cereal boxes sing of adventures untold,
While crayons conspire in heaps, bright and bold.
Every corner of chaos, each smudge and each streak,
Tells a story of mischief, of funny and cheeky.

Beneath the Gumption of Gossamer

Cobwebs sparkle where giggles reside,
A spider in glasses makes art with great pride.
Jellybeans dance in a lighthearted jig,
While shadows play tag with a curious pig.

A bee in a bowtie buzzes through dreams,
Crafting sweet tales full of whimsical schemes.
With a flick of its wing, it sends laughter afloat,
As everything's silly—a comedic anecdote.

The Fabric of a Thousand Masks

Threads of delight weave a tapestry grand,
With clowns on parade and a fairy at hand.
Jesters and jesting in colorful styles,
A quilt made of laughter, a patchwork of smiles.

In the folds of the fabric, escapades dwell,
Each mask tells a story, each tale casts a spell.
With sprinkles of mischief stitched perfectly tight,
Every layer bursts forth with humor and light.

The Secret Life of Stiffened Dreams

In corners where strange hats reside,
Lurks a dream that will not hide.
A top hat twirls on a shoe-less foot,
Singing songs of sugar and soot.

A fedora nods with a silly grin,
While bowler hats invite a spin.
They chat of tales not meant for day,
Whispers of laughter in their own way.

The felt and fabric start to sway,
Dancing secrets in a playful fray.
Oh, the stories that await to burst,
From all the hats the world has cursed.

With every tip, a giggle breaks,
A crown of laughter, the silliness wakes.
Stiffened dreams begin to prance,
In the hidden realm of whimsical chance.

Gathering Clouds in Fitted Form

Round and round the brims do spin,
In a storm of laughter, let the fun begin.
A beanie floats on a cloud of cream,
While newsboys chuckle at the dream.

Pork pies wobble, oh what a sight,
As whispers gather in the fading light.
They swap old jokes, and puns galore,
Each snicker ignites a silly roar.

Fitted shapes in caps and hats,
Join together like a flock of bats.
In fluffy clouds, they hatch their schemes,
To unleash a tempest of funny dreams.

So next time you see a hat in fright,
Remember the fun that's tucked in tight.
For gatherings held in furry form,
Can weather the storm and keep you warm.

The Guardian of Forgotten Dreams

In the attic, secrets softly reside,
A guardian of dreams with a jolly stride.
A hat on the shelf, dusty but grand,
Keeps watch for the wishes unplanned.

With every nibble of whimsical lore,
It tickles your fancy and opens the door.
Toppers and trilbies, a dance on the bend,
Creating a ruckus, on hats they depend.

Hordes of slumber, with stories untold,
Lurk in the fabric of visions bold.
A satirical cap tips, a grin starts to bloom,
As the guardian stirs from its cozy room.

Dreams grow legs and begin to prance,
Swaying and swishing in a hilarious dance.
Each forgotten thought stops by for tea,
In a whimsical world, where laughter is free.

The Craft of Preserved Whimsy

In a workshop, shadows flicker and hum,
Hats wait to speak, making folks go numb.
Crafted from giggles and stitched with care,
Whimsy preserved in a touch of flair.

A beret listens with a cheeky pout,
While sun hats whisper curious doubts.
They argue their merits in silken hues,
Which one is best for a wild excuse?

With pom-poms bouncing and ribbons unfurled,
They plot an escape to a silly world.
The laughter binds them like threads of lace,
Creating a tapestry, a whimsical space.

So raise your gaze to the hats up high,
Each one a portal where giggles comply.
In every stitch, a jest is sewn,
In the craft of whimsy, joy is grown.

Mirage of the Enigma Topped

A whimsical riddle floats on air,
Like socks on a cat without a care.
Cabbages dance with glee and delight,
While shoes serenade the stars at night.

Frogs wear trousers, quite the sight,
Chasing fireflies in the fading light.
Topsy-turvy, the world spins round,
In this puzzle, laughter is found.

Dreams Adorned with Silken Auras

In slumber's embrace, the balloons take flight,
Tickling the moon with joy and delight.
Each dream weaving threads of glee,
As marshmallow clouds sip herbal tea.

Bananas wear boots, oh what a trend,
As gnomes on stilts begin to ascend.
Chasing giggles through the cotton candy,
Where giggling unicorns look all dandy.

A Cap Full of Wanders

A cap that hops and skips with ease,
Carrying tales like a gentle breeze.
With every bounce, a new jest is born,
As lemons play tag in the early morn.

Socks become friends with curious mice,
Spinning in circles, oh isn't it nice?
A treasure trove of chuckles and cheers,
Keeping smiles bright through all the years.

Colloquies in the Hidden Chamber

In a room where shadows play and tease,
Chairs tell secrets with a playful breeze.
The walls giggle with echoes of fun,
While hats debate under the golden sun.

A rabbit recites poetry to a wall,
As curtains sway in a merry brawl.
Cupcakes engage in a dance so spry,
In whimsical moments, we all fly high.

Chronicles Hovering Above the Head

In a world where pigeons plot,
A cap's a fortress, like it or not.
Beneath the brim, secrets unfold,
Tales of mischief and stories bold.

Cabbage hats and silly ties,
A crown for clowns, oh how it lies!
With each tilt, giggles take flight,
What's hiding there? A joke or fright?

Men in bowler, women in fray,
Each hat a joker in its own way.
A dapper chap with a grin so sly,
Plays peek-a-boo with the passerby.

In the breeze, they dance and sway,
Whispers of laughter, come what may.
All hail the hats that cheer and play,
With humor sewn in each array!

Unwritten Textures of Time

A floppy hat with endless tales,
Hiding mischievous little snails.
On windy days, it spins just right,
Bringing forth a laugh, pure delight.

Layers of fabric, stories untold,
Where do they go when the night turns cold?
Adventurers whisper, secrets so fine,
Beneath the weave, comedy aligns.

Smiles peek out from every seam,
Tickling minds like a whimsical dream.
In the shadows, giggles reside,
A tapestry woven with fun and pride.

Oh, what marvels this time has spun,
Unraveled laughter, a joyful run.
In textures old and colors bright,
We wear our laughter, light as a kite!

Brilliance Shielded by the Lid

A beret worn with a sly grin,
It hides the winks from deep within.
Each tilt a signal, each flop a tease,
Wonders await, if you just please.

Silly hats with bells that jingle,
Dancing owls and frogs that mingle.
From fedoras to caps that crop,
Each one's a story that won't stop.

Underneath, a mind so spry,
Like a magician's flourish in the sky.
The brilliance bursts as the lid comes free,
A fountain of giggles, pure jubilee.

With feathered friends and playful crowns,
We spin our tales in joyful towns.
So lift your lid, don't play coy,
Let laughter bloom; it's purest joy!

The Complexity of Woven Whispers

Chapeaus that chatter, a kaleidoscope bold,
Each thread a laugh, a secret told.
Lopsided visions and echoes of grace,
In every stitch, a smile finds its place.

BENEATH the weaves, hilarity brews,
Plays afoot with unpredictable cues.
Tickling fancies, funny just so,
Complexity wrapped, it starts to grow.

Top hats tip in flamboyant glee,
Giggles glimmer, oh so free!
A cascade of chuckles from peers nearby,
As whispers tickle, chaos does fly.

So wear your crown, let the laughter grow,
In woven threads, let humor flow.
For each little quirk that makes you stand,
Lies the complexity, oh so grand!

Unfolding Tales Beneath Twisted Fiber

A sneaky rabbit hops with glee,
His ears wide open, can't you see?
With carrots stacked, in quite a mess,
He's juggling lunch, oh what a stress!

A whiskered fox, a trickster bright,
Snoozes nearby, his tail in flight.
What dreams he spins of tasty treats,
While munching on his stolen wheats!

A turtle rolls by, slow as a rock,
With a hat made from an old clock.
He claims it's magic, gives him speed,
Yet still he stumbles, oh what a lead!

And so they gather, a laughing crew,
In tales spun warm, and laughter too.
Beneath the edge, where shadows play,
Life's quirks unfold, come what may!

Chronicles Carved from Threaded Light

A mouse with glasses reads a book,
He ponders deep, oh what a look!
With every turn, his whiskers twitch,
The words of cheese, he starts to rich!

A parrot squawks, with knowing flair,
He tells a joke, and fills the air.
With feathers bright, and lines so grand,
His punchlines hit — oh how they land!

The cat rolls in, all fur and pride,
With a wink that says, 'Come for a ride!'
But watch your toes, they're quite the snack,
As laughter echoes, there's no way back!

So gather 'round, let stories flow,
Of quirks and laughs, like seeds we sow.
Beneath the thread of sunlight spun,
The fun unwinds, oh what a run!

Arcane Whispers of the Tapered Edge

A jester leaps, with colors bright,
Twirling high, a comical sight.
He trips, he falls, with grace absurd,
And leaves us laughing, not a word!

A wise old owl, with spectacles thin,
Claiming wisdom, with a cheeky grin.
"Maestro of puns," he brags, you see,
Yet slips on branches, as silly as can be!

A playful breeze, it swirls about,
Carrying giggles, without a doubt.
As squirrels plot, with tiny schemes,
The world's their stage, to chase their dreams!

So here they dance, a merry throng,
Amidst the whispers, where they belong.
With jests that twirl and tales that bend,
Laughter's the magic, to the very end!

The Pantomime of Perched Wisdom

An owl on high, with feathers grand,
Hoots softly, making us understand.
Yet as he ponders, he starts to sway,
And tumbles down, what a clumsy display!

The chipmunks cheer, with peanuts to throw,
As the owl squawks, all in a row.
With jokes on paws, they tease and play,
What wisdom there, in their own way!

A hedgehog quips, with spines held high,
"Wisdom's sweet, but oh so shy!"
He rolls in laughter, a prickly ball,
And soon enough, he's joined by all!

In antics bright and lessons shy,
They share the space, beneath the sky.
With each laugh shared, a bond is sewn,
In the pantomime, we're never alone!

The Echoing Gaze from Above

A wide-brimmed wonder waves to all,
Whispers of secrets in the splendor tall.
Dancing shadows leap and sway,
With every glance, they join the play.

A glance up prompts a silly grin,
What's hidden there? A squirrel or kin?
The brim's a stage for cats on high,
Meowing tales as pigeons fly.

Laughter bubbles from the peak,
As the breeze begins to speak.
We laugh about the tales we weave,
In this world, make me believe.

So let's all gaze, in wonder's trance,
While life's umbrella gives a dance!
For beneath this lid, we're all quite mad,
The echoing gaze can't be too bad.

Landscape of the Enigmatic Lid

Oh, the lid, like a mystery dome,
Hiding stories far from home.
A landscape where the strange birds sing,
And laughter loops around like spring.

Beneath its edges, the shadows prance,
Whimsical beasts take their chance.
With jigs and jiggles, they cavort,
In this charming, silly sport.

The sun peeks out, quite bashful and bright,
Wondering if it's day or night.
A waltz of whimsy, in the air,
As laughter curls without a care.

In this realm, where jests collide,
Adventure sparkles, joy won't hide.
Join the fun, lift the lid wide,
In playful realms, let's take a ride!

Of Ribbons and Enchanted Threads

A ribbon sways, so bright and bold,
Tied to stories waiting to be told.
Enchanted threads of laughter spun,
We weave our tales, oh what fun!

Each twist and turn brings giggling glee,
Invisible lines, linking you and me.
A tug here, a pull there, let's not delay,
Our silly dance won't lead us astray.

With every knot, new tales arise,
As playful spirits fill the skies.
From floppy hats to shoes untied,
We giggle and jive, let joy be our guide.

Together we're a motley crew,
With laughter that rings truly through.
So join the dance, no time to dread,
In a world adorned by ribbons, we tread!

Suns and Moons Within the Lid

Suns and moons float in a joyous mix,
Where laughter's the balm, like a clever fix.
Chasing shadows round in circles wide,
In this ludicrous laughter ride.

The moons giggle as they steal the show,
While suns skip past, moving to and fro.
In this zany, spun-out land,
Joyful hearts form a playful band.

Poking fun at time, both day and night,
As whimsical wonders take to flight.
The hat is a portal to these delight,
Binding us all in laughter, so bright.

So raise a cheer for the mixed-up skies,
Where fun resides and silliness flies.
In light and dark, let's find the cheer,
As the world spins round, with joy so near!

The Constellation of Fine Spun Yarn

A tale told by a crafty chap,
With threads and fibers in a map.
He knits his dreams with a wink and cheer,
While everyone laughs, he knows no fear.

His needles click like a castanet,
Each loop and swirl is a love duet.
But oh, beware the tangled mess,
For that's where humor likes to rest.

He spins a story of a lion proud,
Sipping tea, under a bright pink cloud.
With every stitch, the laughter grows,
As curious minds start to propose.

So gather 'round, and take a seat,
This show of yarn is quite the feat.
In every twist, a joke is spun,
In the constellation of yarn, there's fun.

Flutters of a Daring Plume

A feather light, with a twirl and twang,
It danced and pranced, and oh, how it sang!
With every flutter, a chuckle arose,
Amid the giggles, a funny prose.

It wore a grin in shades of blue,
Winking at friends, as if it knew,
That laughter hides in silly grace,
A daring twirl, a comical chase.

The duck in pursuit, oh what a sight,
Bumbling along with all his might.
The plume will tease, the duck will chase,
In this playful flight, laughter finds its place.

So catch a feather, if you can,
In this caper, every one is a fan.
For when it flutters, joy unveils,
In the light of humor, no one fails.

One Thousand Stories in the Weave

In a tapestry grand, with vivid thread,
Lies a thousand tales, all joyfully spread.
Each stitch a giggle, each knot a joke,
Where laughter lingers, and spirits invoke.

A pirate yarn, with a jolly raid,
Chasing after gold, but oh, they mislaid!
With squawking parrot, and pies gone wrong,
In this woven world, we all belong.

A tale of a cat, sly and spry,
On a quest for fish, oh my, oh my!
But when he trips, and he starts to roll,
The audience laughs, losing all control.

So hang up your worries, and grab a thread,
Join in the fun, let laughter spread.
For in every weave, a story is found,
In this world of giggles, we're all spellbound.

Imagined Paths of a Woolen Crown

Upon a head, a crown does rest,
Made of wool and a cheeky jest.
With every loop, a giggling throne,
Where silliness reigns, and wit is grown.

Its edges frayed, with colors bright,
Daring the bold to share delight.
As wisecracks bounce from ear to ear,
In this playful realm, there's never fear.

A jester's feast, where laughter flows,
Tales of mischief in woolly rows.
Each stitch a riddle, a pun, a tease,
In this comical court, we do as we please.

So don the crown, and spin a yarn,
Beneath its warmth, there's no need to warn.
For in imagined paths, we will be found,
Laughing and loving, all around.

www.ingramcontent.com/pod-product-compliance
Lightning Source LLC
Chambersburg PA
CBHW070313120526
44590CB00017B/2656